Gallery Books
Editor: Peter Fallon

THE QUICK OF IT

Eamon Grennan

THE QUICK OF IT

Gallery Books

The Quick of It
is first published
simultaneously in paperback
and in a clothbound edition
on 25 November 2004.

The Gallery Press
Loughcrew
Oldcastle
County Meath
Ireland

ISBN 1 85235 370 8 (*paperback*)
     1 85235 371 6 (*clothbound*)

A CIP catalogue record for this book
is available from the British Library.

Contents

because the body stops here . . . *page* 11

So this is what it comes down to? . . . 13
With a little quick shudder . . . 14
Coming on the burnt-out house . . . 15
As if on cue, the heron's . . . 16
Now the buried stones . . . 17
Soon enough, of course . . . 18
When that great conflagration . . . 19
You wonder what'll come through . . . 20
Off the skin of water . . . 21
From time to time, walking . . . 22
When my daughter begins . . . 23
Bent over his time-polished pitchfork . . . 24
While you're gazing . . . 25
When I saw the deer's breath . . . 26
Skelped, ice-bladed . . . 27
When I see the quick ripple . . . 28
After his lovers run wild . . . 29
Back they sputter . . . 30
It must be a particular kind of grace . . . 31
Did he imagine it . . . 32
Quick now, it's as if . . . 33
Because in dreams . . . 34
After I came across the cluster . . . 35
Insomnia, you say . . . 36
Inside this piebald tinker's horse . . . 37
See what the dust does . . . 38
Although snow has wrapped . . . 39
Hunkered in itself . . . 40
To gauge the scatter . . . 41
I'm trying to get one line . . . 42
Such solidity these stones . . . 43
What happens when a body . . . 44
Light as a feather . . . 45

What the sea does . . . 46
No matter, go on . . . 47
Blood-red, impeccable . . . 48
By leaving always . . . 49
When the small hulking rock . . . 50
Mud-stockinged, stuck . . . 51
A summer of blackened slats . . . 52
Casual, prodigal . . . 53
Rained in all day . . . 54
From the angel of weddings . . . 55
I watch a father . . . 56
Like a drunk sergeant . . . 57
When a heron . . . 58
Working all day . . . 59
Rasp-throated, the choir . . . 60
You might have imagined . . . 61
Touch-me-not wherever I look . . . 62
Because I'm seeing it . . . 63
Even under the rain . . . 64
The hare that takes its time . . . 65
A morning washed to gleaming . . . 66
While I'm hanging out this bath-towel . . . 67
So I keep saving . . . 68
What disappears when I say . . . 69
Deep as it might be . . . 70
Only the shaking daisy-crowns . . . 71
Good to draw the rake . . . 72
When we stood on that brink-bit . . . 73
Whisper of wind . . . 74
Between the river Lurgy . . . 75
Like sweet bells jangled . . . 76
All his life, we're told . . . 77

Notes and Acknowledgements 79

At Half-past Seven, Element
Nor Implement, be seen —
And Place was where the Presence was
Circumference between.
       — Emily Dickinson (# 1084)

         Enough
To believe in the weather and in the things and men
Of the weather and in one's self, as part of that
And nothing more.
       — Wallace Stevens, 'Extracts from
        Addresses to the Academy of Fine Ideas'

because the body stops here because you can only reach out so
    far because the pointed
blade of the headache maps the landscape inside the skull and
    the rising peaks with
their roots behind your eyes their summits among the wrinkles
    of your brow because
the sweat comes weeping from your hands and knotted
    nipples because your tears keep
kissing your cheek and your cheek feels the tip of another's
    tongue testing your tears
because the feel of a beard along the back of a neck is enough
    to melt the windows in a
little room because the toes the thighs the eyes the penis the
    vagina and the heart are
what they are and all they are (orphan, bride, pheasant or
    fox, freshwater glintfish of
simple touch) we have to be at home here no matter what no
    matter what the shivering
belly says or the dry-salted larynx no matter the frantic pulse
    no matter what happens

So this is what it comes down to? Earth and sand
skimmed, trimmed, filletted from rocky bone, leaving only
solid unshakeable bottom, which won't in the end give in

to the relentless hammer, whoosh, and haul-away of tides,
but stands there saying, *Here I am and here I stay*,
   protestant
to the pin of its terminal collar, refusing to put off the sheen

of its sheer-scoured surface, no widow weeds in spite of loss
after loss, whole wedges of the continent, particles of the
   main
plummeting from one element to the other and no going
   back

to how things were once, but to go on ending and ending
   here.

With a little quick shudder the bushes part and offer to my
    eyes a wren

that stops there, seeming entirely intent on the strains of
    Mozart's
Symphony 29 — composed by a boy in love with Italy, as the
    wren's
coal-speck eyes are in love, it would seem, with that splash
    of light

brassing the grass, and with the scarlet dazzle-dangle of a
    fuchsia skirt
with purple lining. It is that nib-specific *focus* I'm seeing in
    the bird
and hearing in the music, the in-lit contingent presence
    things hold

in the moment to moment passage of their happening, the
    wholehearted way
they're in a state made up of bristling force and chaste
    patience — which
stars have, and wind-twisted sycamore leaves, and the seeds
    of lightning.

Coming on the burnt-out house, he wonders what to make
of the wells he finds in the fields around here, their walls

scummed with moss, beetles swimming in their frigid
green depths, not a drop drinkable till a hard scouring

happens. Ruined stone, a rusted padlock, nettles hemming
broken glass: fire that took the life of the place has left

such signs of flourishing decay. With steel brush, shears,
and a fresh-polished vessel, he'll begin the business of cut

and cleanse. Seeing clear water in the earth under him,
he'll bend to the next task, building from the ground up.

As if on cue, the heron's a rising and gliding apparition,
    casting no shadow
on the packed snow I'm running over, morning under cloud
    a dull grey
ache. Frigid air's taken in at the mouth, to mix with the
    warm world
of tongue and palate, gums at blood heat: it informs with its
    frisson of chill

the spongy honeycomb of lungs, and lives a few expansive
    instants there
before turning like a swimmer and journeying back and out
    into frosted air
as a quick wisp of steam, the sign of my being here and now
    — as that heron
tilting between branches is here and now, taking air in and
    letting it out

as he angles through it and over the rise and out of sight,
    seeking a safe
still fluent place to feed in peace, before this cold un-homes
    everything.

Now the buried stones have risen and would almost talk
to me; now the tall hawthorn by the gate keeps making these
snaggy passes at me under my dome of shouldered hay; now

nimble blood has dried to my mud-caked knuckles, leaving
two small crimson badges signifying nothing except the fact
I can't handle a slash-hook the way my neighbour can, who
    slices
fuchsia and briar to a neat avenue of clean-cut branches; and
    now

the bees have taken over again the dark world above my head
where they lead incessant, single-minded lives, boiling in the
    attic —

isn't it time to step from shelter, breathe the free air, and say it?

Soon enough, of course, the eyes adjust to this huge absence
    in which
trees begin wintering, their colourcd draperies given over,
    leaving

naked shapes, ramifications, a reminder of what's at the
    heart: a going
away, the brilliant vertiginous vocabulary of leaves, of
    being-in-leaf,
stripped down to sheer unmitigated syntax, this sense that
    what begins

in anchorage and rooted thickness will taper till the endmost
    twigs are only
hair-wavers wincing in air, tiny cleavers of light, solid
    shadow-nothings
of live wood reaching out the way wiry white tendrils of
    roots go groping
down in the dark. Now
                    emptiness is all, and you may read
    what this late
radiance has left in its wake: signs — stark silent — saying
    what's what.

When that great conflagration had finished with us, I sat in
 the silence of rocks
angled exactly against the gale that was still swallowing air
 from the southwest
and watched — on a cobbled stretch of sea bleached green
 and streaked by
stripes of navy blue — two big loons sitting calmly on the
 swell, unruffled
by the blast, out of range of that passionate self-immolation
 that was the surf
dashing itself against black rocks, a white mane riding its
 buckle-crown of green
and turning to a fleecy nothing, a salt collapse, then
 resurrection as grotted air
where scattershots of rainbow shards kept netting light, to
 which these
peaceful birds pay no attention, going at intervals under
 and staying there,
then breaking back to air again, glancing round to glimpse
 each other, settling.

You wonder what'll come through the cracks you've papered
    over
now forsythia, magnolia, all the short-lived brightnesses
    begin
their shining.
                    Voiced like mourning dove and motorbike,
    great whales
moan underwater lullabies, love songs; and all the old-world
    words
like *husband, wife, spouse* — gleaming like new leaves —
    mean
a walk across patches of trespassed grass.
                                    Beneath the
    chestnut's
candelabra, the slow-bowling arm of the campus worker
    bends,
broadcasting seed in a clean line.
                            Chill days: you sense your
    skin's
been lifted, leaving soft raw flesh to feel these shifts in
    weather, its
tart reminders; taste seething flux, tomorrow's foggy salt.

Off the skin of water scumbled blue a ghostly steam-mist
    rises, as the frost-
chilled air kisses river surfaces and something changes.
    Something changes
when two outsides touch like that, each sensing the touch of
    that sudden other,

as something changes when our wrists and fingers settle and
    slowly stroke
each other, taking time to savour the way we feel what's
    happening here:
the cool of skin meeting the under-heat that blood is, and
    answering

its delicate imperative with this smoulder-burn, this
    elemental shift from
earth to air and what begins to feel like fire, as if a ghost of
    soul shimmered
above the skin we share, the way those wavering radiant
    exhalations now

curl their incessant ghost-shapes off the skin, air-kissed, of
    river water.

From time to time, walking through the fall morning — sky
    a pale
blue diorama streaked with cloud, the ghostly half moon
swaddled in cloudswirls — the inkling of a dead animal will
    wrinkle air

so I'll wonder what it is and where it's lying, the mass of its
    matter
only matter now, hardly mattering, opening the busy mouths
of earthworm and spider, diminutive jaws of the ant, the
    beetle's teeth

ravening to bring all flesh to grass. But there's a live crow
    now —
dark legs stalking across a gutter that glows in this light
    coppergreen:
it dips, drinks, snaps a seed that's flown to rest. Still I can
    smell

the dead — till darkwings open wide and rise, cutting things
    off.

When my daughter begins to talk logic, murmuring over and
    over such open secrets
as *Law of detachment, modus tollens* and *disjunctive
    inference* (the big words, it seems,

making her mouth happy) I find we're standing on another
    threshold, and see
her recede from me into the quiver-thicket of her own life, its
    zigzags hidden

so I can't follow her to the heart of where she's going,
    leaving me in the middle
of this dark wood, though still in earshot of each other — so
    even if she won't see me

here in a splash of accidental light, she'll hear the words I'm
    saying and the way
I say them over, getting them by heart, sending them after
    her into the distance

she's starting to be now, learning to be her own language,
    from where
she'll send back bulletins (reports, coded probes, quick
    proofs) to find me.

Bent over his time-polished pitchfork, my neighbour who's
     turning hay
in the big wind blowing off the Atlantic is the moving hiero-
     glyph
for *Man-who-belongs-here* or *Two-hundred-years-ago*,
     which is also

the sign of a local tree, the sycamore baring its pied bark and
     giving
leafy tongue to the air's passage through it, that long run-on
     sentence
trembling toward its final verb which can be days coming,
     during which

one invisible blackbird goes on making music, becomes an
     inky swirl
on shadow-paper, a sounding heart in the heart of uproar,
     a brushed text
that would say, could we see it, *High wind: morning all
tossed about* —

his incendiary yellow-ringed eye running rings out to the
     rings of Saturn.

While you're gazing in the mirror all the names change.

It will all be all right, you've said, when push comes to shove
and the snow's sheer mortal diamond will have left us
its legacy of watergallop and what-have-you: it will be, then,
a question of reflection, not this heartlessness of lightbreak,
horrid jag-edge of shadow.
                              Take, for instance, this morning:
beneath the ice-clamp of Casperkill Creek you saw clear water
run into its own life against the odds, making (the way things
will) a fresh start — just as a raucous, high-minded, truth-
    telling
matter-of-fact congregation of crows comes tumbling.

When I saw the deer's breath enter air and burn there — each
exhalation a puff of distant gunfire, the animal stopped
    foursquare
and surveying me, her ears upright and brindled like a hare's
and swivelling to any sound — I remembered what the
    plumber said

about the seven-point buck he'd been (with his hunter friend
who'd *taken it down* with bow and arrow) butchering.
    They'd opened
the soft white belly with knives, he said, and let the creature
bleed — *It's what you do* — and bleed. Of course he could
    only

stomach so much meat himself, he said, though he liked it for
breakfast sometimes, in sausages. *Spiced*, he said, *and fixed
    up nice.*

Skelped, ice-bladed, fairly scarified by this gale with hail in
    its teeth,
you keep seeing the rainbow in the belly of the storm and
    you want

the work — though it won't be all things to all men — to
    have myriad
instances in it: gale, hail, rainbow, the way these ice grains
    hop off grass

and how your cheek feels, being struck, not to mention the
    dark-headed
running plover, the yellow petals of gorse that signal some
    new *now*

to grey, February-naked air, or the stream so over its stone
    causeway
it can't be crossed and you have to turn back the way you
    came, turning

the other cheek to hailstone and wind-nip, bearing the brunt
    of weather,
learning what *storm of circumstance* really means, and *winds
of change*.

When I see the quick ripple of a groundhog's back above the
  grass, its earth-
brown pelt vanishing into a hedgerow which for a minute or
  two is a shaken
screen of greens and then again still, the creature melted into
  nature's mouth
and sending back no sign of itself though I know it's in there
  and I can sense
how its breath and broadly distributed embrace of its gaze
  have become so fully
what it inhabits it will even winter there, curled round its own
  heart beating
at quarter speed, at ease in the sphere of its own immediate
  knowings — then
for some reason Avon's native comes to mind, quill-end
  tipping his tongue
as he takes a breath and disappears into the leaves and lavish
  music of another
turbulent little word-shiver for a minute, and he is all alone
  there, listening.

After his lovers run wild in the woods of midsummer, the
    known world
turns upside down for a space and nothing is as it should be:
    infidelity

only a sub-set in the major species of uncertainty, of
    instability at the core —
the way light and shade keep changing places or how the
    weather races

from thunder, lightning, a downpour suddenly deep-
    drowning the air,
to clear skies and starlight, the eroto-hypnotic flicker of
    fireflies

fuddling midnight, the sheer persistence of things in spite of
    how the tide
keeps flowing against them. And is this why, after a maze of
    meanders,

you find yourself back at a high window, eyes scrabbling
    glass, waiting
as a watchman might wait for the far flame to blaze or not
    blaze out?

Back they sputter like the fires of love, the bees to their
    broken home
which they're putting together again for dear life, knowing
    nothing
of the heart beating under their floorboards, besieged here,
    seeking
a life of its own. All day their brisk shadows zigzag and
    flicker

along a whitewashed gable, trafficking in and out of a hair-
    crack
under wooden eaves, where they make a life for themselves
    that knows
no let-up through hours of exploration and return, their
    thighs golden
with pollen, their multitudinous eyes stapled to a single
    purpose:

to make winter safe for their likes, stack-packing the queen's
    chambers
with sweetness. Later, listen: one warm humming note, their
    night music.

It must be a particular kind of grace, the way this wild
        morning a family of swallows
is harvesting the cloudy air: harnessed to its wheels and
        pulleys, they harness

the blast to their own advantage, or stop on it for a second
        before letting its breath
take them where it will, their small streamlined bodies abroad
        and at home

in its hugeness, their screams carried off so I can catch only
        the faintest trace
from where I stare out the kitchen window, wideawake to
        these tiny life bundles

in daily negotiation with the great unnameable force that
        lives in things, the way
they're beyond complaint, too busy living to be bogged or
        beaten down for long

by sudden swerves of weather; beyond even contentment;
        having only this instant
quick knowledge the moment gives them: and how to go
        on, making the most of it.

Did he imagine it, or was that her shadow standing solid
    against the light —
what the French call *contre-jour* — a body darkened by
    daylight the way
the body he was seeing in the slow-dawning twilight of
    brightness
was an outline with thickened volume, no fine detail visible?
    It could easily
have been a shrub, a stone bench, a fencepost, any upright
    repository of shade
under a luminous half moon and a scatter of stars starting to
    vanish as the sky
lightened silvergrey to chalkblue where he walked by the
    small lake in which
the moon floated among the black triangles of trees, their
    hemlock selves

near enough to touch, real as the crows making for daylight
    quarters
or seven deer processing, like pilgrims, their solid shadows
    through the garden.

Quick now, it's as if air had bared its bright teeth: snow petals
blowing so everyone stops to stare a minute at the last flitters
of winter come among, then sun again, as if the season's
   drunk

on its own manic fast forward — as a couple on bumpy
   ground
will swerve between humours, their talk now fire, now ice;
   sunshine,
then rain quickly following; cloud that in an instant clears.

But what are those creamy yellows breathing in and out at
   the end
of maple branches? Haven't they heard? Are they deaf as
   posts —
and all their seed, breed and generation — to what happens
   here

where we've to live, nature or no nature, keeping our own
   score?

Because in dreams sometimes I've been in so strange a place,
   I wake
as a soul might waken after death, into a space so totally
   unknown

she must pause to take her bearings, knowing the place so
   alien
she'll have to feel her way — bereaved, but for what? for
   whom? — all

the past a blank till she passes an old couple who stir a slight
   vibration
as if known once: he with his stick, she in her cream raincoat,
   they

with their stately early-morning gait; but without the dog,
   the old, slow
shadow that would keep pace with them and briefly lift its
   head, heraldic,

to any stranger. Going by, the landscape goes strange again:
   water, trees,
a migrant bark of geese. *Where is the life I've left? Its sleeping
   statues?*

After I came across the cluster of chamomile, its tidy yellow
    buttons springing out
of a ditch in Clonbarra, and beside it a heal-all with all its
    purple liplets open, a crown
of unexpected light in the rain-soused morning misting down
    from Muckish; and after
I saw the melancholy of wet sheep penned in a field of rushes,
    thistles, scrubby grass,
and observed under dripping sycamores a long-legged black
    young heifer standing
and sending see-through bursts of breath to hang an instant
    on the rain-laden air —
I couldn't but think that in the heart of things, at the very
    centre of what's possible,
a kind of patience is the way we manage; waiting in our own
    way till the days of rain
lift, a few rips of blue appear, and the darkened field lightens
    all of a sudden
to purple, mauve, gold, and yellow-amber; to asphodel, eye-
    bright, heal-all, chamomile.

Insomnia, you say, is good for me. Unloved by sleep, I fly
    wide-eyed
to wakefulness — into a dark that isn't so black then, letting
    those
ghosts from the exiling light enter. They're not entirely
    welcome

night visitors, though one of them is no dream at all, is
    maybe — come
to think of it — the only true one among them: that
    remembered red dress
fluttering empty sleeves; blackboard, desks, a clock on the
    wall. So

we close the door and wait. Nothing doing: suitcases
    everywhere
and I can't find my shoes. Tears, then, and a change of light,
    seeming
to empty the air of air. Dumbstruck suddenly, faces flat
    against glass:

out there the world, its wildflash mirages. The room sick with
    waiting.

Inside this piebald tinker's horse a prince of steeds
pawing to be free; makes it as far as those fiery eyes
that blaze behind a matted forelock of tangle
to look out at a world they can only look down on,
ears still rampant with the clamour of battle.
                                        Blinding
the dazzle of the here and now, perpetual gallop
from ice to steam and back, brazen hold-up of clouds,
till their heaven-hammering descent darkens everything.

So you'll bow down to grass. You'll take its tame scents in,
barely showing your teeth to them. You will bend the knee.

See what the dust does when the sun — just risen for its last
    lap — raddles it
through and through. It glows. It's a million mullion-bits of
    radiance
blinding him to all the ordinary stuff, to trees and passing
    traffic, even

to his child leaving for school, her mother disappearing in a
    haze of blue
through the hall-door, the cats in their cave of sleep, middens
    of Christmas
gifts in corners, dishes in the sink. There's nothing to be seen
    of any of it

once these dust-brilliants become the living world and all he
    knows is
torched, scorched to ash-scald by this apparition, though all
    can still make
good, make estimable sense. But nothing (livid quick bliss it
    signals)

strikes home as the dust does — leaving him deaf, dumb, blind,
    bedazzled.

Although snow has wrapped the house in a quicklime bandage
six miniature daffodils in their earthen pot have begun to
    blossom
and (if I lift my eye from the cloven signs of deer) the redbrick
    wall
and the tall chimney of the Powerhouse are bright worldly
    things
against the backdrop of weather turning its back on us.
    Dark water

under a shelf of snow; stark sycamores a dozen crucifixions.
    Stepped
up to its belly in snow, the cat watches some bird or famished
    mouse
make its own cold life minutely happen.
                                    But what are four
    small oranges

peeled and placed on a starched tablecloth of snow a sign of?
    Being
a gleam of something — not consolation exactly, but still
    mattering.

Hunkered in itself, tiny eye blazing, the wren vanishes as
    they all do, as the redbreast
did in its blackened nest-pyre: just a walnut of char I'd
    turned to ash so the wind
would take it, and the rain in shiny fat drops rinse from the
    rock its poor remains,

or as the fox cub did, which stopped, curious as any child,
    and stared at me
where I'd stopped to watch it scramble the bank by
    Kylemore — its pelt
a light ginger, its face marked charcoal, its white-tipped tail,
    its eyes pooled
to an infant's speculative intensity, everything being seen for
    the first time, wanting

to know what had stopped like that, what animal I was, what
    emanation of the day
or sudden creature coming out of the weather. *What are you?*
    was its innocent gimlet
probe of the world's body — just hungry for knowledge —
    before it melted into hedges.

To gauge the scatter of reflected light Bonnard pinned silver candy-wrappers
   to the studio wall. Imagine how his two eyes took coruscating jag-angles

off that crinkled surface, how he sipped it for some corner of shade between
green and violet, or for a grid of crisp yellows configuring the big window

in which an old mimosa tree waves the brain-levelling brightness of its own
Bonjour! Or for those brief thumbnail streaks in which he painted, late,

his own raw torso and the scurfy triangle of his domed head. Silver sweet-paper,
its magpie glitter: how he wants it at the end in his flowering almond, seeing

Green, bottom left, not as it should be, needs yellow, and with a friend's hand
helping, he touches the spot, very gently, to glow gold-yellow.

I'm trying to get one line or another right when a flock of
    starlings startles —
mobbing a marsh hawk, staying up-sky of him, folding round
    him their net
of black silk till he shrugs them off on a downdraft, the whole
    flock closing
like a broken concertina into leaves where they become
    invisible, only throats
crowding the air with clamour.
                              Meanwhile the hawk is
    elsewhere, hawk-brain
beating to another music: in the great blue hush of space, he
    pays attention
to the air itself — a live feather-tongued light-rush bearing
    him up, droll wingbeats
opening and closing it like breath.
                              Invisible loonybells, the
    starlings go on
chattering their jangle-life in branches, telling me how my
    own head won't
let go its appetite, is an old knife on stone: bitten blade,
    handle bandaged.

Such solidity these stones have, rising in rose, russet, soft grey
    and sandy colours
to be library, music hall, or chapel. Struck or settled on by
    light this morning
they make us feel their weight: how anchored they are, all
    their glass rectangles
catching quickfire; how their arches stand witness to the
    wedding of dark and light
on the perfect pause of thresholds.
                                    Not the fierce fragility
birds are: robins, waxwings, starlings that cluster along eaves
    or swirl about
the slate and copper rooftops, or gather in bare beech and
    sycamore branches
whose last leaves drift in the no-wind and land so soft on
    water they cause no
circles, are tiny boats fraught with light: not solid things but,
    like your breath,
desperately there — warm, no words in it, nothing to build
    on or be sheltered by.

What happens when a body is thrown open like a tree the
    sun rummages
and light lies on each leaf like a tongue of fire or a scalpel of
    pure edge,
brightness honed to so sharp a blade it goes through things
    like an act
of transubstantiating sight, the way you once thought God
    could see
inside your soul?
                        At times you may feel like that, flayed by
    the way
you're looked at by eyes your eyes have entered headlong,
    dragging
what's left of you along with them.
                                        Flayed: the quivering skin
    peeled
and what's under it exposed, slowly, the way this maple tree
    is losing
its mantle of leaves, and the truth of treeness starts to be seen:
    tangleswarm
of janglenerves; scars; wrinkles; all the hard stuff shivering
    from the heart.

Light as a feather the way he slipped away: nothing
of Oedipus in it, no thunderclaps of applause
as the old man goes off-stage into mystery. It is

the silence after, though, that has to be the same:
slipping into everything, lying between one nature
and the next, or falling as it fell last night at dinner

when the three of us in a lull of talk put our elbows
on the table and sat watching the candle flicker a little
in the crosscurrents of our breath, one breath coming

in silence after another, lost like that, light as a feather.

What the sea does — coming, going — is mole beneath the
    seeming solid earth
and keep eating at it till it gives over at last its stony hold on
    things
and another chunk comes tumbling.
                                What's strange is, after
    so many years,
I've never seen it happen, never been present at that pivotal
    single instant
when these two (solidity and flux, the rooted and the rootless,
    ruthless
flowaway heart of the matter) meet and mate for a moment
    — a moment

in which sea-roar and land-groan become a single deafening
    sky-sound
before that jawing withdrawal, collapse, that racing after, so
    foam, stones,
churn of sand, swirl of seawrack make a wrecked mouth
    bulging with one

loud clamour-tongue, which the rock you stood on plunges
    into, dumbing it.

No matter, go on, while the little rabbit engine of the skull
keeps drumming the end thing and, arse-up in creek water
half iced-over, the ducks are making kittenish sounds,
and airborne geese (mandarin eyes cast down) figure on the
    wing
their landing chances.
                    Here now, still warm and looking
normal, it's only the heron's glazed gaze and unfazed
    stillness
give the game away, say his bronze lemon splayfoot will lift
and settle no longer in swamp or stream in such a silence

that the frog or vigilant fish could know no more of him
than of any branch or stone stuck in mud or kissed by water.

Blood-red, impeccable, these tulips nod to us in the sun and
    say *Drink!*
That big tree — sycamore or London plane — is it a huge
    household for songbirds
in summer, or simply a great maker of shade, a master of
    blue air?
                Of all the geese
that moved over us, shouting their bone-joy at change and
    restoration, only one
couple stopped at this small lake and laid a family down, so
    now three yellow
black-beaked balls of down shiver in the grip of clamorous
    instincts and read
what secrets the low weeds hold, while their parents stick
    out strange tongues
to hiss at us.
                Over its own shadow, an ant carries a seed in its
    teeth, scuttles
under the shadow of the mute dove rising from a mound of
    dead leaves
and jumping into sunlight — a self-shaken thing, live as a
    heartbeat, blinding me.

By leaving always a single stem and a leaf on one Seville
    orange
Chardin fashions a lesson in framing — that spear-shaped,
    green
and slightly curled form fixing a clean limit to each
    composition

in its lovely huddle of apples, goblet, pear, two soberly
    corked
wine bottles, one nut, a solitary flat-shelled clam. Possible,
    too,
he may have been attending to the way live nature stays

at the given edge of everything, a real presence even in these
absolute indoors of the eye, the orange's opaque radiance
still trailing and displaying its tree-life, its one last longing

attachment to sunlight, *plein air*, everything out of the
    picture.

When the small hulking rock on my path along the early
    morning dark started
to be the skunk it really was and waddle an undulant shuffle
    away from me, showing
its chiaroscuro self by the luminous leftovers of a full moon
    and stars, I startled

for a second or two, brought up short by the uncertain
    solidity of a world that keeps
falling back to a fluency that's just the simple fact of things
    being plain as day
and enigmatic — that clear core we say we see in *Being* being
    merely the *opaque* itself

but seen without its mask for a moment, telling a truth clean
    as the swoop-lines
a suspension bridge has: such stolid mystery they make, and
    we walk on water. Water
is like that, hitting the back of your throat with nothing but
    its wet cool, nothing

in or beyond it — distinct as the invisible dawnbird or a voice
    inside a voice, informing you.

Mud-stockinged, stuck in the mud in front of their byre,
the heifers are making low moaning sounds

as if something deep inside their collective heifer memory
were rising to greet the weather they've been standing in

for days, for aeons of days — all the cloud caravans off the
    Atlantic
unloading their water-haul here as they've always done

and no end in sight. It's the mud of ages they're helpless in,
listening for the metallic rattle of the gate, the dry *whissk* of
    hay

falling in front of them, the squelch of wellingtons. Mournful
as monastic leftovers, they bow to it, won't meet each other's
    eyes.

A summer of blackened slats, murder of bees, stale perfume,
and in the dripping leaves off-stage where you wait to go on
there is this low whimpering.
                                    But when you have done some
small thing — filled feeder to brimming with millet and
     sunflower,
and a chickadee hops near your disappearing thumb and
     perches
and proceeds to eat, and the zip of daylight hisses on
     wingflicker,
and a bell sounds from God-knows-where and it's nothing
     you know
and gone sooner than it takes to say *This happened* —
     still it did,
you know it did, you felt whatever it was, and even the weight
of that past tense can't quench the quickened life it had in it.

Casual, prodigal, these piss-poor opportunists, the weeds
in their gladrags and millennial hand-me-downs
of yellow and purple and pale green, are everywhere
along the highway, on every inch of waste ground
in our cultivated suburbs where they raise their families

and squinny in through lace-curtained windows, wagging
their heads at us, flaunting their speechless force, their
eager teeming in themselves, the irresistible fact that
theirs is the kingdom, the power, and the glory
of the real world smiling full and frightful in our faces.

Rained in all day like this, I keep towelling the windows dry,
trying to wipe the fog away that has me blind behind glass,
unable to see the world outside for what it is, how things

become shadows and blunted silhouettes of themselves, birds
only blurs where they shake a branch when they land or leave
or just dash past, a flash of cloud-particles snatching at crumbs

as I do myself each time I get the big window clear again and
    try
to take in all the shapes and colours there, all those living bits
of matter that stand in their own ordinary uncanny light

until blearing begins again, and I see my own breathing does it.

From the angel of weddings to the line of washing over-
    floating
an alleyway is a short walk, so I imagine those big wings —
    raised
to bless whatever comes down — casting a clean shadow
    across
frocks and shirts and underpants arced as a rainbow over
    cobbles,
that marble messenger from elsewhere and the everyday
    radiance
of these stay-at-home signs of the world's surface coming
    together
for better, for worse, splicing spirit-bodies to each other in
    the daily
communion of light, closing the common distance between us
in this city where every step is a sort of walk on water, a
    litany
of unlikely beliefs, the mundane amazing at ease on every
    corner.

I watch a father teach his twin sons to play tennis, and see
   how vividly
in it they are. *Too late*, says Petrarch, *to live tomorrow; you
   must*
live today, while late afternoon daylight is flying through the
   postcard

pinned by my window, giving a momentary umber glow to a
   Chardin dish
of plums, a bottle, two cucumbers, a half full glass of water.
   The fruit
is a smoky navy-blue, the bottle onyx, the water see-through,
   and those
cucumbers keep a faint oatmeal luminosity to sheen their
   squamous skin.

Like the father brushing up his boys' back-hand, the still life
   is alive with
the light of the moment I'm sitting in, knowing only the lack
   of it, the day
disappearing as yesterday's egret did, in a green otherwhere
   of shadow.

Like a drunk sergeant, death stalks about the house
kicking the furniture, and everywhere you look are trees
just lopped, their trunks barely showing overground,
a thin glitter of wood-dust making glimmer-rings
around them.
    Felt absences. Bright dust
solid in circles.
     Nothing to be said, it seems, or done,
though small points of scilla prick out, breaking the brown
scurf of leafmould, while windblown-by-March daffodils
in huddles incline pale faces to the light.
         Green stems
take it hard; unaccommodated selves are shivering.

When a heron, that protected bird, and a windhovering hawk
    appear
framed in the one window for a minute, as the bigger slowly
    flaps
towards Tully Mountain and the other does its Nijinsky trick
    of standing
on air — wings so fast they're like a long sentence out of
    Beckett, energy
immensely expended on going nowhere, shaping up for the
    kill — I don't

only remember the heron folding and unfolding itself over
    Omey Strand
when we spread your mother's ashes on the water and I said
    An image
of eternity (though *patience* must be what I meant), but think
    also
of the small heart hiding in heather-tufts and hoping — breath
    by breath
and smell by smell — for another instant free of those lethal
    eyes, then another.

Working all day to draw one tongue into another, chasing
    word-mice
through cluttered cellars, I'm trying to hit a right note, bring
    over

what the man said to make one or other of his lovers shine
like the necklace he saw splashing into a reed-pond — its
    gleam

of beads at speed like the flare of a bird's fire-fangled dovetail
taking off. Or it's the glint of insect on apple catching his eye

in a greenhouse steamy with the scent of sex and lemons, his
    blood
beating its drum to kingdom come. So I keep at it — like a man

entering an empty house, who tries to fill the place with her
dusky smell, warm breath at his neck, her *Where are the
    words?*

Rasp-throated, the choir of insects and tree-dwelling
    amphibians sing their single-word
anthem: *Autumn*, they chant, and *Autumn, Autumn*, while
    overhead the moon — Her
Royal Phosphorescence — sits arbitress and casts my shadow
    where night secretes me
in one of its occult corners and I am eyes, footfalls, this long
    deep humming in the head.

Mornings, though, I've become such a normal creature small
    birds pay no attention
to my passing, the still brilliant moon still buoyant in the early
    blue above my shadow
where it crosses the shadow of trees and stops when the deer
    lifts her head from grass.

Only the width of a path between us, I can count the
    modulated staves of her ribs, see
the white line of spittle flecking her nether lip when she goes
    back to browsing. Then

I vanish into air all effulgence, as if a pearl were ground to
    powder and flung about in it.

You might have imagined when the two collared doves sprang
    out
of that cottage shell abandoned long ago by the stricken
    builder
that the spirits of two fugitive lovers had found their way to
    wings,

so the sight of them hightailing in a flash of white and rosy
    brown
towards the shelter which rocky groves in the foothills of
    Tully provide
might have given some kind of consolation. And it did for a
    minute

bring a smile of surprise, only broken by the sight of all those
sally trees turned brown, bitten by a tiny screw-shaped
    caterpillar
into plague-signs among summer's other flourishers.
                                                    Brushing
both sides suddenly like that, how can your steady step not
    falter?

Touch-me-not wherever I look — its tiny orange cup and
  spur curling or spitting seed
if I brush against its frail green stem while running myself
  into the ground here

where students have begun to saturate the space again, their
  ripe bodies shining
from every corner, travelling singly, doubly, or in packs,
  their youth a raw burn

against the season I feel in my depths: arms, bare legs, the way,
  like brazen water,
slick shoulder blades and back muscles ripple, greased and
  made sleek by the clean

sweat-film that gleams there. So I learn the cloud-lid on life,
  again, *is full of rifts*
of glowing light, and may even lift to let through an eye-
  hooking slash of blue —

as a woman in a summer dress riding a bike will let the silk
  ride suddenly up
in no breeze but her own motion, and her thigh is alight
  there where your eyes are.

Because I'm seeing it from behind the fine mesh of a
    window-screen, the tree
spreading beyond my second-storey window has a slightly
    fuzzed look, as if
each of its leafy branches had been badly rattled and all its
    leaves had
shaken themselves into frazzled clusters —
                                    the way Corot
        sees them rising
beside a glaze of water, a kind of off-key radiance agitated
    by a painted breeze
and billowing inside an atmosphere that is, or seems to be,
    a perfect marriage
of plain air and water, its coupled elemental life a quiet
    interior shining, that
sheen of water so clean you can't say if it's moving or not, each
    leaf a blurred

but still distinctly living thing in which, this minute, a
    flickering black flock
of starlings has settled and become, no matter how hard
    I squint, invisible.

Even under the rain that casts a fine white blanket over
    mountain and lake
and smothers green islands and soaks grass and makes a solid
    slow dripping
trickle in the sycamore; even under the rain that's general all
    over the valley;
even under the steady rain measuring my life perched beside
    the big window;
even under the blank remorseless grind and colonizing
    hegemony of rain —

the bees are out among the furled or flapping scarlets of
    fuchsia bells, seeking
till they find a fresh one, then settling and entering,
    gathering what they need
in deliberate slow shudderings of the whole body shaking
    suddenly the honey-core,
then extracting themselves in silence, a little heavier, limb
    filaments glinty,
to go on cruising through this dust-fine deliquescence of
    damp the falling rain is.

The hare that takes its time crossing the drenched garden
and stopping to nibble little bits of what takes its fancy
doesn't know the news I've gathered from the newspaper
I was crumpling for the fire this storm-unruly morning,
and neither does the clackering magpie or *tikketting* wren —

while the wind that shakes the barley and the bare branches
hasn't heard a word of it, although it stops me cold
and on my knees like this, staring down at the calm
light of her face and mischievous amusement in her eyes
shining up at me among the lives of the freshly dead.

A morning washed to gleaming skin and bone, to the vapoury
    radiance left
by rain, to such absolutes as my own shadow burnt in tree
    bark and hedge leaf,
living its other life there while I walk its present provisional
    body towards

the vanishing point, peering back to see a small fleet of ducks
    muckraking
the grassy verge — for earthworms, I guess, whose thirst has
    brought them out
to savour the aftermath of last night's downpour, blind
    blood-coloured bodies

sliding through raptures of damp, through the palpable slow
    ecstasies of drip
and slobber, smells of freshened earth their paradise as the
    ducks peck at
and swallow morning's manna — a gift to give thanks for in
    an anthem of quacks

as they waddle a swamp of sunlight — totally for the moment
    and at home in it.

66

While I'm hanging out this bath-towel, the colour of
    blackcurrant and claret, it flaps
like a prayer-flag and brings back the sunbursting gale that
    blew the three of us
out of Mannin Bay and into the grassy dune where we lay
    to picnic on salted
tomatoes and the finer salt of sand in the cheese sandwiches,
    and heard the wind

clatter across rocks between us and the shoreline, and felt
    safely tucked away
until Kira made me stand on a steep rise and hold between
    us the big towel
swelling like a spinnaker, madly crack-dancing, a live sail
    trying to take us with it

though we stayed — unsteady on the edge as we were —
    grounded and holding our own
against the weather, its pitch and fling and drag snatching
    our laughter but leaving us

half air-creatures, and you reclining there like a sand-nymph,
    one weather eye open.

So I keep saving the bees taken unawares by glass,
shrouding their music in a bundled dishcloth till I shake
it out outside and they float off over the fuchsia hedge.

So the moths that flutter up from curtain folds and out
of the sleeves of old sweaters are fingersnapped at
to become Ash Wednesday stains on my handskin.

So the snail is lifted from the sand, laid on wet grass,
and so the yellow cat in my dream is stalked till it turns
to a lean woman in suede leaning in to me. So who

handles all this? Lays all of it out? Keeps the reckoning?

What disappears when I say the word *bird*? That little thing
  all shades
of brown and raspberry and rose on my windowsill: clicking
  bill, a feathering

that raddles light; depthless black reflecting eye; a syncopating
  bulge where
heartbeats harry the breast; the swifter-than-eye-can-follow
  side to side flick

of the head? I can hear its distinct twittervoice. *Finch*, I say,
  getting
a hold of it. *House finch*. It doesn't move a muscle. Then a
  branched robin

fan-batters charcoal wings, and I see before it disappears its
  burnt-orange
breast, an ember blown to brightness by the cloudy morning,
  and I almost

feel it as the quick blink of God's one eye, the eureka-brisk
  surprise given
and taken, the *echt* unmanageable absolute of it in the moment
  passing.

Deep as it might be, what is our silence to the silence of the
    village of Slievemore,
its upstanding stone skeletons open to the blows any booming
    weather off the ocean
can throw, its grassed lanes and main street given over to the
    air since hunger

struck, laying them low, hunting the shawled and barefoot
    villagers onto the road
towards the boat at Louisburgh, the long haul to Newfound-
    land or South Boston,
their old home a haven now for gulls, a hawk or two, some
    gannets plummetting

among the rocks, who'll weather there, sitting out the storm's
    ferocity? And what
is the little edgy chill that lingers between us to the great freeze
    that folded snow
and cliffs of ice over most of the island, though it left one
    corner free to be itself —

so strange shapes of land and stranger flowers settled there
    and became native?

Only the shaking daisy-crowns of fleabane mark the
    groundhog's trail as he flows
down the riverbank cloaked in wet chokecherry and
    anonymous foliage. The doe

and her two fawns — stopping to stare before gingerly
    stepping through underbrush
and raising small puffs of water-vapour off dark myrtle
    leaves and the curved leaves

of Solomon's seal — are wrapped in such silence I can
    almost hear their eyelids open
and close, their ears swivel and dip, silk-quick grace of their
    limbs shiver to attention,

ready for flight. Mushrooms have sprung overnight out of
    leaf mulch: they gleam
like moonrocks or shards of icefire, taking root among dead
    things of earth, the lush

mothering leaves a ground for them to glow on, taking over.
    Light, under the green
dome of my umbrella, is a celery shade in which, like startled
    carp, my eyes tread water.

Good to draw the rake through cut grass: dry wisps catch in
the plastic
yellow tines, make a scratchy sound as they gather and you
shake them off

and reach for another rakeful, your movements slow,
deliberate, steady
as rowing. Good when the live grass comes up clean and green:
you see

the neatness of it, how it shines, starting life again in the free
air, letting
light stroke every slick blade, sleek-shining from its time in
the dark.

Caught between satisfactions of rhythm, sound and sight,
you see this is how
what you want to say may come clear as you revise (rake the
dead away,

bring the living to light), till you find under a tuft of cut grass
a wild bees' nest
which you cover again, seeing its tiny golden honey-eggs
blaze by daylight.

When we stood on that brink-bit where rock, sea, sand and
    grass
touched each other, stood on a prow of stone shouldering
waves foaming over it, I knew how separate father and
    daughter
were, how her self she was, how that stage of the journey
    was over.

With wind in her face and a faraway look in her eye, she
    seemed
free of all my fret and hover, sufficient to herself, ready to meet
(I could almost hear her '*Let be*') whatever might happen,
    to take all

in. I let her be like that, then, feeling it, and went back to
    looking
at what the waves were doing to the stone mass we stood our
ground on: how heaviness rose, cracked, broke, becoming
    light.

Whisper of wind in the grass, among leaves of the ash: *Settle down,*
it says, *there's lots more where this came from.* So can it be we're just

a clinker of dust, a swirl-whirling rock-dervish, a series of lucky breaks
or unlucky happenstances? Somewhere in the unfathomable shadow

of spacetime, out there in the blind and airless dark, a herd of miles-
wide rocks gallop like circus horses round and round and round

in crazy circles: manes of fire; eyes gouged out at birth. Nobody
cracks the whip, though gravity keeps them in decent line until one

salmon-senses the real absence, makes a run for it, leaves the rest to
our imagining: the coming home of the odd chance of it — it happening.

Between the river Lurgy and the Leannan, just outside the
    village of Estrin,
there's a cluster of small houses, brightly painted, and a bed
    of flowers edging
the road I'm travelling, at the sight of which a sudden
    emptiness full of light

is what I become, as if I'd had a glimpse of something no
    words fitted,
but unmistakable as radiance — a halo shaping itself round
    the walls of these
neat houses and around the flowers blooming in the shelter
    of wet hedges

and round the rain as it fell in fine drops on the heads of
    four sand-coloured cows
lying like icons of patience on the grass, jaws meditatively
    munching, their eyes
open to the wind and rain of another ordinary day in the
    green world between

the rivers Lurgy and Leannan, just outside the tiny,
    centreless village of Estrin.

Like sweet bells jangled in a minor key, starlings make in the
    big sycamore
their autumnal music. Invisible from down here, their throats
    are open

to ripeness in the air, its *mellow fruitfulness* and that slight
    musky edge
which may inflame them to this rhapsody of rapt cacophony,
    this annual tribal

intoxication of the larynx that won't stop fattening, falling,
    improvising
one fleeting tune from their collective heart. Each year I hear
    this concert

that goes on for days, as if the whole congregation had taken
    leave of its
sober senses, taken its note and cue from some soul hymnal
    — a dark choir

of voices tuning, turning to flame, a harvest of bittersweet
    orchard chords
saved from summer, pickled a little, offered up now while
    there's still time.

All his life, we're told, *Chardin struggled to overcome his*
    lack of natural talent,
so I begin to look again at his olives and peaches, at that cut-
    open cantaloupe
with its orange innards on show, or that orange from Seville
    he kept giving
a bit part to — to burn softly in its given space, to weight
    the picture in a newly
luminous way.
                Or how the dead rabbit's fur is a dry gleam of
    white at the heart
of warm browns, or the way each feather in the dead red
    partridge is a live thing —
the bird's life stilled to this final exposure of itself.
                                                    The
    struggle you see is with
the facts themselves, and with some knowledge he kept
    hidden from our eyes, some
unspoken sense of how *there* these bodies are, and nothing
    can say it the way it is —

only you look again, stretch your hand, dip the bristles, risk
    again the failing stroke.

Notes

page 13   The phrase in italics remembers Luther at Wittenberg.

page 29   The reference is to *A Midsummer Night's Dream*.

page 36   This poem is in part a translation from a short, late poem by Montale.

page 47   The phrase in italics is a mistranslation from a phrase (*n'importe allons*) in a poem (*Une Vie ordinaire*) by the French poet, Georges Perros.

page 56   Petrarch's words come from his *Secretum*.

page 59   Many of the images are culled from various poems by Montale.

page 62   The phrase in italics is borrowed. Having mislaid the source, I'm unable to give the author due credit, for which I apologise.

page 73   *Let be* is Hamlet's phrase.

page 76   The phrases in italics are from *King Lear* and from Keats's 'To Autumn'.

page 77   The italicized sentence is from Pierre Rosenberg's *Chardin* (1963).

Acknowledgements

Acknowledgements and thanks are due to the editors and publishers of the following magazines where many of these poems first appeared, in earlier versions: *The Antioch Review, The Clifden Anthology, Five Points, The Gettysburg Review, Green Mountain Review, The Hudson Review, Irish Pages, The Irish Times, Lumina, Metre, The New Republic, The New Yorker, Pelagos, Poetry, Poetry Ireland Review, Poetry London, Quarterly West, The Recorder, The Shop, Solo, St Ann's Review, The Stinging Fly, Stride, The Threepenny Review, Vallum, Washington Square* and *The Yale Review*.